S L I P

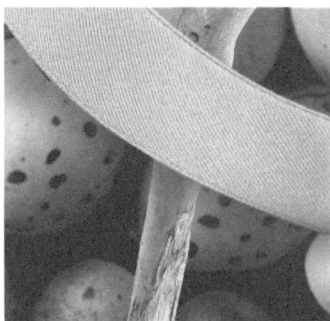

NICOLE CALLIHAN

(Sb) **saturnalia** | B O O K S

Distributed by Independent Publishers Group
Chicago

Saturnalia Books
2816 North Kent Rd.
Broomall, PA 19008
info@saturnaliabooks.com

ISBN: 978-1-947817-76-0 (print), 978-1-947817-77-7 (ebook)
Library of Congress Control Number: 2024948851

Cover art and book design by Robin Vuchnich

Distributed by:
Independent Publishing Group
814 N. Franklin St.
Chicago, IL 60610
800-888-4741

Contents

I wandered through a house of many rooms.
It grew darker and darker,
Until, at last, I could only find my way
By passing my fingers along the wall.
Suddenly my hand shot through an open window,
And the thorn of a rose I could not see
Pricked it so sharply
That I cried aloud.

—Amy Lowell

The Stick

There was a stick at the mouth of the cave.
These are the things I did with the stick:
chewed it, waved it to the sky, poked myself
in the eye, pretended it was a daisy, pretended
it was an orchid, a tulip, lily, cigarette,
made it into a gun and shot my brother,
nudged my brother to make sure he was dead,
nudged my brother to make sure he wasn't dead,
licked it like a lollipop, sang into it like a microphone,
brushed my hair with it, brushed my tongue,
gagged myself with it, gagged myself again,
made myself throw-up, made myself cry,
made myself look pretty, made myself
sit in the car alone, made myself practice
writing my first name with the last name
of a boy I loved, whipped my knuckles with it,
my thighs, dug little stars into my forearm,
tried to beat off a man, tried to beat him harder,
tried to use it as a megaphone, tried to pry
my mouth open and say the words out loud,
made it into a Calculus equation, an airplane,
a gun again, pointed it to the sky,
prayed over it, moved to Brooklyn with it,
took it to the bar, punished it, ignored it,
pretended it wasn't mine, put it in the corner
of that dirty little apartment on 12th Street,

let the cat piss on it, wrote bad poems about it,
slept with it, let it touch me in places I had never
been touched, let it scratch the very itch it made,
took it to a candlelit dinner, packed it up into a U-Haul,
turned it into an altar for my wedding,
danced with it instead of with my father,
took it on my honeymoon, didn't breathe a word of it
to my husband, shoved it to the back of the junk drawer
in our new home, forgot where I put it, searched for it,
found it only after I forgot I was looking,
let it accompany me to the hospital, bit on it
while the baby was being born, bit on it
while the next baby, the sick one, was being aborted,
bit on it when the littlest was born, tried to prod myself
awake—my God, I was tired, all those years of nursing,
of thermometers and backrubs and mommy,
mommy don't go—started sleeping with it
under my pillow, took it to therapy, gave it a name,
hid it behind my back when my husband walked in,
danced with it, wrote it an inappropriate email,
wished I had buried it by the mouth of the cave
when I still remembered where the cave was,
used it to call my mother to see if she remembered
the cave, turned it into a peace offering, until finally
I tied a string to it and dangled the string into the river.
There, after one thousand years, I caught a fish.
But the fish was too small, so I threw it back.

girlhood

after we emptied the house of men
we let the curtains grow dirty
and tore numbered pages off the wall
I carried a stick Heather a brush
we ripened in our weeks-worn swimsuits
and sucked our mouths raw with fireballs
on the most special night of the year
we'd get a port wine cheese ball from Krogers
and make a pallet on the floor
lock the door dip our fingers
into mother's Fuzzy Navel as Miss North Carolina
floated from one side of the stage to the other
she was our dream one day we too could have
a safety-pinned sash and talent shaved legs hope
we would be far away so grown and loved

On the Second Day of the Third Decade in the 21st Century

I tell the children the same story two days in a row.
It's about the past, how I used to think it was the future.
You told us this yesterday, they say.
In the past I told you this, I say.
My husband says I walk around in my nightgown speaking nonsense.
Four or five times a night, I go to check the children's breathing.
If that is what I am checking. Is it?
Days, I hard boil eggs, fill ice cube trays,
leave bags of razors outside the yellow wooden door.
A jigger of black coffee and some chicken skin for breakfast.
The scrape of the fork in the bowl. The loneliness.
I tell the story again, this time with my nightgown pulled over my head.
I shake my finger at the sky. One day you'll understand, I say.
My own mother is in the driveway. She waves.
My brother, who is in the tub with me, pushes the paper boat my way.
We'll never be like her, we say. Never, never, never.
As if never could be nailed to the wall.
I turn the pages of the calendar.
When I was little, I thought this was the future.
We know, we know.
But now it is the present, now the past.
I was so little. A glimmer in a blind eye.
My father's hand on my mother's thigh.
In Soho, there is a place called The Earth Room.
Two weeks ago, I went and stared at the dirt.
I am back there now. Back. There. Now.

I sit on the floor eating chicken soup.

The soup is very hot, but time moves, so it cools.

Suddenly, I'm like, OH, I CAME FROM THE EARTH,

AND TO THE EARTH I SHALL RETURN!!!

This is a revelation. I laugh. Do I laugh out loud?

I don't know. I'm all alone.

You are not allowed to touch the dirt in The Earth Room,

so I do not touch the dirt, but god, I want to.

I want so badly to touch the dirt.

Maybe I will climb into the dirt?!

I will yell to the children to bury me in it!

Bury me in it!

Like a day at the beach with mother!

When I leave The Earth Room, I hear the blood in my ears,

which also I hear now. Does everyone hear this?

And what do the razors even *mean*?

What were they even *meant to mean*?

And where oh where is mother going?

And why oh why would anyone make a boat of paper?

My God, woman, pull down your gown!

twenty

there was rice
in the saltshakers
I married

the ketchups
rubbed spots
off silverware

mostly wore
my hair down
back then

or didn't but
remember it down
kept my money

in a sock
only had a fan
still prayed

mostly I saw
windows flying by
a little snow

if you dropped
pennies in me
you'd hear them

hit the bottom

How We Flounder Here on Earth

The tang of state fair dust
on my ankles and my shin
burned by Ricky's tailpipe,
out past the heather fields
and bowling alley; past
Jimmy's shack where he sat
like a monk, his ground beef
browned in a cast iron,
his too-young girlfriend
blushing in her tiny shorts,
her pretty freckled arms
crossed over her chest.
Past, too, Mama Heaton's
room with its peeling ceiling,
and all the days of someone
else's life silent on the tv,
past the fellowship hall
and the Jello, Brother John's
wide face, his pockets fat
with penny candy, and who
was I? A child. A pebble
crammed into a crag.
An incongruent marionette.
An avatar of who I'd become,
who I became, who then
became who now becomes.

I didn't yet know how
I'd become undid, undone.
What's hard won. The pink bear.
The misheard. Squall of living.
If cleanliness is next to godliness.
That little girl with her dirty nails.
The snitch and stench. Then
being known is a sort of heaven.
Meet me out back, past
the lilies and the righteousness,
the mushrooms in the commode.
Show me what is yours,
and I'll show you what I call mine.

Morning

The light from the kitchen is a square in the field.

An empty truck in a gravel drive, idling in the gray.

It's always been my favorite time of day.

I can almost differentiate the hum in the walls from what's inside my body.

In the city alley, a cat in heat.

It's been so long since I've heard this sound.

The howling, the calling.

And these kitchen lights: squares in the squares.

Driving out to the farm with Frank, there was a breach pony.

We drank our coffee from blue tin, smoked cigarettes with holes in the filters.

Now, a siren.

In my mother's kitchen, the second hand—ticking and ticking—but never pushing past the nine.

Or going out to walk by the ocean.

Before the sun comes.

Before the earth turns just so.

I am not sure who I belong to when I sleep.

But morning I feel mine.

My dad worked third shift. I'd be up and waiting when he got home.

We'd share a bowl of Cheerios before he slept.

Then you only have one bowl to wash, one spoon.

It's sleeting on the skylight.

The cat has grown quiet.

How nice to have sturdy walls, windows that open and close.

How grateful I am.

And I would like a spoonful of almond butter.

My grandpa stayed up so late and woke so early, they became the same.

My favorite color is the exact shade of his coffee.

And the ash in his tray that was the gray of the not yet day.

And I would like other things, too.

But there is not much you can get before dawn.

Or maybe everything is the same before dawn and after dawn.

It's a naming thing, a shadow thing.

The way there is one light that won't wake the others.

The way, eventually, except once, they'll wake anyway.

True Story w/ Horse

In the dream, you came to me. The barn was a barn I fell asleep in as a child, or drove by years later, milky-eyed from days of road, or it was just the grasses where a barn once stood before the fire tore through. Do you remember the fire? There is so much to consider and re-consider. In the dream, you cracked me open with your fingers and ran your thumbs across the wound I am. The sky of the dream was a dream sky. Under it, we swelled and swallowed, as the gnats flew into our eyes, and the flies buzzed our ears. From the well of you, I drank, and drank, until drunk on sweetgrasses and rainwater, on the skin of the inside of your wrist, the glass tin pails, horses of copper. And if I had not dreamed all this, I would be sure it was a dream, and my sleeping child self, under rafters and wool, would turn and settle, and hours later, waking, she wouldn't remember anything for decades.

103 Pine Ln.

My mother who though she was not herself an eater of crackers in bed often brought a ginormous bowl of popcorn which she would eat undaintily like just a fistful of popcorn shoved near her mouth the way I eat popcorn unless I am not alone which I do not really prefer and always in her other hand was a novel usually a thriller never a romance always either a woman killing several men or a sister stealing another sister's kidney or a surgeon purposefully botching a heart procedure and I would be at mother's side also fisting popcorn and reading the big horoscope book because there was so much information like what would my sex life be with an aquarius or why to avoid earth signs and also career how according to the stars with my attention to detail I should be a phlebotomist or an instructor of ballerinas and sometimes I'd bring her a warm washcloth or I'd be hungry and she'd say just let me finish this chapter or there'd be one of those magazines with famous people and even of the mildly attractive famous men mother would say well I wouldn't kick him out of bed for eating crackers and I'd imagine that flat paper face fat and fleshy in bed with us a couple of sleeves of saltines and the crumbs different from our hard little kernels and then I'd go into the kitchen and stand at the sink hollowing out the strawberry stripe of the Neapolitan before checking the windows for strangers. There: my glassy face, the indifferent moon, the treeless street.

The Origin of Birds

For hours, the flowers were enough.
Before the flowers, Adam had been enough.
Before Adam, just being a rib was enough.
Just being inside Adam's body, near his heart, enough.
Enough to be so near his heart, enough
to feel that sweet steady rhythm, enough
to be part of something bigger—it was all enough.
And before the rib, being clay was enough.
And before clay, just being earth was enough.
And before earth, being nothing was enough.
But then enough was no longer enough.
The flowers bowed their heads, as if to say, enough,
and so Eve, surrounded by peonies, and alone enough,
wished very hard for something, and the wish was enough
to make the pinecone grow wings; the wish was enough
to point to the sky, say bird, and wait for something to sing.

some psalms

*

like bread I eat ashes
my soot mouth   my root
my throat clogs with you
Mother says it's okay
to say all the terrible things
butter   rain   yesterday's pain

*

at bright center night
near of burning things
and you on the stairs
the bees too the songs
sorrow and swelling
and yea though I walk
have lord mercy on me
my eye also my throat
and my belly your voice
in my palm   my heaven
my balm

*

for my lowly pouring out
his plea   for my lowly
pouring water the pitcher
blue my lowly low
poring over the words
faint his call   pale prayer
holding sustenance for all
the horses of the earth

*

feels like rain but no rain
I dreamed we were dying
eggs in juice glasses
this immutable anguish
these affectionate afflictions
languish me with language
my bones waste away
o lord are you risen yet?

*

I quake and may offend
may offended be but
the heart in the body
on the bed is still   still
the heart is in the body
on the bed   a spoke
a sprain   a stroke of rain
what I speak is spoken for

*

all morning estranged
from the sun   a hand
on my face   flat palm
wrinkled   sheets   what
the throat catches it holds

*

in heavens and also
grass besides you whom
else do I have do I have
you even you I have had
mushroom skin smooth
this bird blue and the hunger
beneath so many skies

*

I am a dread to my friends
bright night I walk streets
barefoot   I am animal
in the city   am shame
in a ballcap   the neighbors
pretend not to know me
and they don't

*

like water I spill out like
water you run me until
I am clear   I am never clear
in darkness you place
your finger inside the glass
that holds me gulp me
at the sink   your thin wrist
to shut the faucet   storm
swarming   still parched

*

that swath of summer
when clouds stream water
the bolts and bolting
unmade steam unseemly
I was but still I seemed
though seeming is not
being is not beating
around or near but inside
the bright burning bush

*

roar of your waterfall   surge
of ancient depths   I skimmed
shallows   seawater pooling
your ankles   thighs   that place
of breaking   how you break me
the tender skin unsunned
rope unhung in the pail of sky
break me   break round
what's broken   I am drowned

*

sigh becomes song
I swim in my bed

*

with fingers and thumb
you held open my eyelids
and I beheld you
behold still   be held
I throbbing could not speak
but throbbed and throbbed
everything was known

*

this heart hot within me
my thoughts of soot
and steam to speak
with the tongue is to
say the folds of my brain
hold your body still

*

yes on my couch I recalled
you   I recalled you on my couch
what feet in my lap   what head
in yours   the night-watches
so persistent in their counting
the hours licking the nape
of necks   o lord on you I dwell

*

the depths themselves
shuddered   shuddered depths
and also shuttered   also
screened-in   as in
I would like a porch on which
you could read me poems
that tremble with whatnot

*

under wing and pinion
I pluck feathers and pine
what faith   what buckler
the buckled   unbuckle
my shield and rampart
my truths wander in
and out of their small rooms

Diction

What would *be the right word?* He asks. I hold the question in my mouth like a hard candy, suck it 'til my tongue is raw. Yes, *what* would be the right word, or *why* or *how*, or *who* might be the right word, or *you*. Try *pomegranate, rain, rifle*. Listen, the only time I ever held a gun it was yours: I fired it into the dead of midnight sky. That's a lie. There was another afternoon when the sun was an arrowhead, and I couldn't stop shooting Cheerwine cans off a barbed wire fence. I keep thinking I'll die, but instead I wax my uncomely privates, heat up fish sticks, try to find the right words for things. I write words I don't mean, say words that are mean, catch my daughter writing words that aren't right. *We don't say* this *word,* I tell her, even though we do and have and will. In the dim of the kitchen, she starts ripping the paper in pieces and placing those pieces into her mouth. *What are you doing?* I ask. *Swallowing them*, she says. *Stop it,* I say, *you don't have to do that,* but she nods her head. Finally I join her, take a shred into my own mouth, taste it, work it with my weak jaw. These are our true and terrible words. Eat them.

Summertime Sundries

1 oz almonds, coffee (black).

On the outside, the apples looked fresh. Cut into them, and they're bruised.

Woke up having bled on the sheets. Outside: mist and birds.

Clean the ceiling fan; make hair appointment; don't eat too much.

I worry that come September Eva will have forgotten how to read.

The nostalgia police were flashing their highbeams.

I thought it was a dream, but it wasn't. The deer just ran off.

"She had a hungry face."

Eva sends a letter to Gaza & Israel. *Find peace,* she writes. *Or come to New York. You should hide closer to God.*

Maybe the Pink Ladies will be better.

What should I tell the monsters?

If at one final grasp at youth you come off as sooooo middle-aged then you are sooooo middle-aged.

If there are drive-through prayer shacks then you don't have to leave your car.

If self-pity is a lipstick color then my lips are ruby red.

"I borrow someone else's form what else is a body?"

An old book on wasps and grace: our marriage isn't the problem, you're the problem.

Of course other people think too. I just don't know about what.

1.5 ozs almonds, an apple.

Before bed I sat in the hammock and listened to the stars.

The yellow house is a place of forgiveness.

If you don't have anyone else to forgive, then you can just forgive yourself.

The pimple on which I put the toothpaste has disappeared.

There is forgiveness and disappearance and a squirrel.

Thinking we should serve pinwheels. Eva wants a piñata. Am I too old to swing a bat?

We don't want to be lonely, but we are.

On the last page of every book the baby proclaims THE END.

If endings were so simple I wouldn't need water.

Remember how the body goes?

Fox-glove. Thigh-high weeds and the boys who pull them.

The friend of a friend who went by the name of an animal.

In the country, I suck Diet Coke back like it's my bitch.

But what of us who are bubbles?

A single room in the mansion of self, a sensitivity to touch.

I think there is hope if only because there is repetition in you.

I want a signature scent that is not too powdery.

When I feed the girls fish sticks for dinner, I feel virtuous. Really, I do.

Though I can spell, I can't make a decent cocktail. No. Really, I can't.

If I do, promise you'll lock me in a pretty cabin.

Maybe the moon is different in Montauk. Maybe the moon in Montauk is different on Instagram. Maybe Instagramming the moon on Montauk makes you different.

Had I remembered the hole, I wouldn't have stepped in it.

And then we started again.

The truth is somewhere between the new light bulb and the burned out one, and the truth is: that was the hardest pill I ever had to swallow.

He says, Everything ok? I say, yes. The children are screaming. There is a shadow and a rabbit, and I'm hungry. Alright then. Alright.

It made a lump in my throat for weeks.

But I find the mumbling mesmerizing.

I refuse to put popcorn into another poem. To put something into your body, ad nauseam, is one thing. To put it on the page is another.

The things we put into our body and the things we do not.

There will be cake.

1 slice ww toast, 1 tbsp miso paste, ½ avocado, coffee with almond milk

Let me check with my husband and I'll get back to you.

Excuse me. Are those jellyfish?

Though it was a beautiful home, it didn't work out because of the pedophile next door.

The neighbors. Fences, flowers, foxes.

My God. Everything is like everything.

Again.

Gin.

Make the bed; shake the comforter; plump the pillow; that's it.

This shit is so simple.

Eat one ounce of almonds; read a blog about self-care; envision yourself as a self-care bloggist; tell people to eat almonds; tell them in a pretty font; insert picture of almonds here: XXX.

I like loose, soft clothes and potato salad.

I like me.

This is the good sober life.

These are the cloth napkins.

It's easy to disappear.

On the promenade there was a photograph of a mother and her child in a cave.

Hashtag refuge.

Hashtag recovery.

Hashtag this is the soul's migration in language.

We'd like to shift the d in dead Mike to a cap; i.e. Dead Mike.

To hide me from your timeline is forgivable. I would probably hide me too.

Not waving but drowning; not cooking but smoking.

I make a mean macaroni casserole and only smoke electronic cigarettes before noon. You?

Q. Why must we have cookies flown in from France?
A. Because they are so good, and they taste like fancy perfume.

You are neither good nor do you taste like fancy perfume.

Oh stop, I'm not so bad. Just thirsty.

Listen: your only task for the party is to hire a lifeguard. The last thing we need is a pool full of dead babies.

Okay, okay. But who will get the hats?

True Story w/ Giraffe

Ella was coloring the most beautiful, abstract thing I have ever seen. I said, that is the most beautiful, abstract thing I have ever seen. No, mama, she said, it's a giraffe. Of course it is! Those eyes, those ossicones, those spots! I am often mistaking things: my mother for a saint, strangers for familiars, my husband for a manhole. One morning, I walked in to teach my 8 am class, and my students were electrons. I traced their particles in the lights. Emma: a loop! If you trace something for long enough, it makes you dizzy; you lose it in the double slit. Even with the clouds I do this. I point to them and say, that looks like a ship, and then, suddenly, I am halfway across the Atlantic: my stepfather clangs his spoon against a glass, the pool is cold, the captain is kind. If things were what they first appeared, then nothing would be as it is.

Time

Of all the social constructs, I think
I love time best. How this morning
which I could call morning I did morning
things, shuffled around in my morning
gown, had not woken to a morning
alarm, because my body is like *morning*
every day come morning, so no need
for an alarm, light through a window
will do, or not even light, the threat
of light through a window will do,
and my body being my second favorite
construct, or having been my favorite
construct when it was young and favorited,
though now I think my favorite favorite
of all the constructs is language. I like
how if you hold a page at a distance
it can say any old thing, but come close,
and I might be offering an image, say,
of my mother on the top of the stairs,
or at the bottom of the stairs, the top
forty years ago, the bottom, only three.
So I guess I'm thinking about written
language as a construct. Anna used to tie
her books in yellow ribbon and carry
them in a basket on her bicycle. I love
remembering her in the village. I love
how we suspected she and Sebastian

were lovers. I less loved when her husband
hung himself in the garage, how she changed
her ribbon to a gray one. Didn't she? Do you
love me, and if you don't, why have you read
to the bottom of this page? It's evening
now, or not evening, but the sky is so gray
that the afternoon seems to be evening.
Is loneliness a construct? Snow? The soup
simmers. After I eat it, will my hunger
be a construct? And if I don't? What then?

Twenty-two

In that I was a baby poet then
with dust in my teeth, the sweetspire
of my mother's yellowed slip,

having been a virgin, then a bornagain
virgin, then born again and again,
the pinkish drool, synovial fisttonic,

I'd write *you, you, you*, and drag you,
darling, through the pond's wetweeds,
sky and stamen, short of breath,

a little note to self, little selfsong
about stone boats, a kiss on the throat,
rootswitch and buttercup, and mygod,

how easy desire came, how easy
the petals in the gutter, the cockpilfer
and rain. I stained the sheets

of all the pages with thisandthat,
dahlia and twine, it's June, and what
I've not deleted, ash and knucklebone,

I know by heart, not tired, not yet,
of being brave, come, come, comeclose,
closer still—of this life, let's have our fill.

Aging

1.

I have been feeling like nothing

A drone outside the window

The Rothko that goes black less black blacker

Hair in unwanted places

In the board book a bear in a canoe searches for food

My daughter makes words in the steam of bathroom mirrors

I always forget until I try to burn myself again

If there were a fire my husband would save us all

Afterwards we will clean the berries and eat them

This must be enough

2.

How willfully I took the apple

How I thumbed the dime in my pocket

Our responses were casual

There was beer to buy

I didn't know if the postage was sufficient

Or if the mind was

The body is another story

Three elevators were broken

There were only four

Eight if you counted the children

Spring is not just something you step into

I had grown fat with winter

Nothing was fair and that was okay but only to those who shined

The skinned knee spoke volumes

The empty milk carton said more

One girl had lice another had pubic hair

Everyone was ashamed

3.

The table was set

But the universe was expanding

We had no bread

Only a vague understanding of our inadequacies

To feel the whole fill the hole

A black dog is not usually a black dog

It is hard to be everything

Similarly hard to be nothing

A drunk a whore and a mother walk into a bar

Pass the potatoes she says

4.

The lilacs smelled like lilacs

A boy read a map on the stairs

In the dream I had cancer

You told your wife

The knowledge made her kind

The kind of knowledge one wants

We didn't know what would kill us

On the train platform I watched the rats

Zoë says oh dear instead of fuck

I fickle and fume and finger the flowers

Eva says I never get mad

5.

From what I remember there were horses in the snow

The common bird was less common

A roll of nickels mattered

If mattering matters

If mothering is collected in the child's behavior

This morning we dyed our hair purple

I coughed up the moon

If the moon is a lung

Who will I disappoint next

Or in whom will I be disappointed

Or where to anoint this disappointing crown

6.

On this very street it rained

Because that is what happens in May

I may always be wrong

An object controlled by physics

The force of two bodies

If this is to this

My mother's lover is friendly

My husband likely wanted a son

Most lives are dull

Duller than a dollar Ella says

But I think she's just talking about sound

7.

How much was it the bleeding

How much something else

How much is always saying

How much is that doggie

How much the window itself

How much the mango

How much the reprieve

8.

Interference between the wings increases drag

Wine glasses fill with rainwater

An umbrella is not a cane

In a pinch most things replace others

I meant what I said

I forget if I actually said it

Mostly I remember your youth

Here the sky is both lighter and heavier

I embarrass myself with the contents of my bag

Feeding you oranges makes my skin sag

Biologists say trees are social beings

9.

By youth I mean mouth

The scholar asks me what I write about

So you're not a Buddhist she laughs

Can I bring you anything else he says

It hasn't occurred to me to be other

Opening the window allows for air

The streets remain unchanged

I have left my family and for what

A murder of crows

10.

If what is unimportant is as important

As what is important then I will

Buy seeded bread   grapes   baby cheeses

Imagine all things are real

It is the least we can do

The air in the room doesn't move

Eventually bodies don't move

For the moment I watch them writhe

For every word you have I have a dollar

11.

It seems late for an apology

You can slide me under a door

Snow comes in through the keyhole

The rain begins again

I keep wandering to graves

Tilt toward meaningfulness the book says

I lay on my side

I sleep with a pillow between my knees

There are many embarrassments

I hope at least to keep my teeth

12.

I have locked all the windows

The clock is louder than my breath

An online quiz guesses I'm 70

Because I eat eggs I think

I walk through the streets

I am not nearly as lonely as you

It's been days since I washed my hair

I don't even know what bird mesmerizes me

13.

My arms are very long

The light is very good

Probably I want to be burned

I don't like to take up too much space

Is that your face

Poets often write about rivers

I'm not sure what runs through me

14.

The potatoes were served with cream
I sleep with running water
The black spot can be washed
Will anything good come
Are water and fire opposites
What is a plum opposite
I keep thinking
I will live forever
I also think apples are good
I have mentioned two fruits
I have said I so many times
What else can I offer

15.

Afterwards we cleaned the berries and ate them

There was a fire

My husband saved us

A bear in a canoe is a silly bear

Shame was a ribbon she wore on her neck

The Rothko gets black less black blacker

A drone flies outside my window

I have been feeling like nothing

This must be enough

Burrow

My mother says the sound haunted her.
She thought an animal had crawled up under her bed
and that it was hurt. Every night for a week,
the whimpering woke her. Mornings, she reached the long hand
of the broom underneath the dust ruffle but came out clean.
The pillow where her head had rested was wet. *So wet*, she said.
As if I'd been crying all night long. But then it stopped.
The animal, wherever it was, had nursed itself well. Or died.
It would be years before we found anything resembling a body.

Beachcombing at 44

Blood on the beak of the seagull

That I am too much and not enough

The lapsed thing laps the shore

Blood on Ella's knee

A pelican in the sea

I write notes to put into bottles

That the bottle holds me

I wave, am waves, am waving

A thousand things I can't capture

The day's catch

The fish is still alive

Blood but for how long

That the pulling back is the rush

If the waves are everything, then everything is breaking

Hymn to Life

The wind rests its cheek upon the ground and feels the cool damp
And here, so early as to still be dark, the windows gray, my robe,
Half my head, some portion of my heart. But a hymn beside a hymn,
Blue beside blue, blow by blow. There's been no weather to speak
Of. No snow. Yesterday, a few flakes, sleet. But nothing sticks
Save a flash of memory or three. I took the train to the east village,
And walking up the stairs, the sun had come. Sometime between
Brooklyn and Second Avenue everything softened. Somewhere?
It was like leaving the matinee and finding day. Buckets of roses.
Purple tulips. When I moved to New York that's all I saw: the fruits
And flowers. Mangos in winter. Delis and deli-men. You could
Put a dime on the counter and take a lime. Then June, when
Everyone peels off their clothes. Layers. August, they disappear.
Then so their thing: to live! To live! So natural and so hard
So hard and so natural. A cultured pearl to bite to see if it is real.
No, the shell is the hard, natural thing. But the pearl. What's inside.
I spoke too soon, then yesterday became the day before. When
The dark gave way, and the windows brightened, I found snow.
Snow on the red car, the blue, snow on the silver, on the blades
Of what's left of the grass, on the blades of the wipers. Blades
Of the few brown leaves still left on the sycamore. For months
There'd been a mylar balloon in the branches. Do you remember
And if you do. If you do. Is that the string still? The golden
String tied to a child's wrist. Ella lost hold of one once in the wind.
I waited for her devastation, but she was unmoved, watched it get
Smaller, up and up, until it was the size of the moon, a thumbnail.
Freedoms at twenty, a relief not to be a teenager anymore. One of us
Imagining the other's devastation. One of us not so devastated

After all. The candy cigarette that was only a candy cigarette. Plume
Of smoke. Someone's chimney up the street. A match in a cupped
Hand in a city south. I let myself sleep until the vault of sky shifted
To day. Or didn't, but let myself sleep so long that when I woke
I needed to fill this or that thermos with this or that food. Hunger
Assuaged. Or, anticipated hunger assuaged. Went to the Whitney
Yesterday. There'd been a green comet the night before. Did you
See it? Haven't read if it could be seen, only read that it would be
Able to be seen. Hopper in the city. Squares of light. Women looking
Young and out windows. Men drowning in highballs. I liked best
His letters to his mother and the sketches which were to become
The thing, or become the thing which best represented the thing
—The world is all cut-outs then—and slip or step steadily down
A sketch of a sketch. A photograph of a body once inhabited sent
By a body briefly inhabited. "There you are." Or once were. There
You once were. Transtromer: "All sketches wish to be real." But
Do they? Is there a box beneath your bed? Around what
Have you tied a ribbon? Hopper's wife shall forever gaze down
At Washington Square. I keep thinking I should water the plants
But know the only way to keep them alive is to wait until they're
Almost dead. No fuss. No finger in the soil. It's gotten so cold
As to make a liar of me. The space heater, dripping faucet. Leaving
The museum I looked for a postbox, got so hungry I ducked
Into a diner, ate tacos, asked a man reading a book with a yellow
Jacket (haiku, tr: Bly) if I could take his portrait, and did. What now
To do with this image of a stranger? Coins on the countertop.
In which the past seems to portend a future which is just more
More of the same, yes, but more of the more, of the fires burning

And not only the controlled burn, but yes the controlled burn,
The sacrificial letters in the campfire. My uncle who used to light
His bills on fire and throw them into an old oil drum. That hill on
Which I was raised, on which I stood. Funny to imagine our child
Selves walking along railroad tracks, our child selves staring up
At the sky. Open field. Heads resting on a skateboard. The moon
Full the way it was full back then. Felt like I'd never seen a moon
So full before. Not funny funny, but. Now full again almost fifty
Years later, and it feels like it's been hardly a week since the last.
The accumulation. Waxing and waning. I don't even say, "Look,
Look at the moon." Or if I do, who hears. "Look, look." 4 am.
Couldn't sleep. Or can't. Hot cinnamon tea. I left the dog in bed.
Another day for each day is subjective and there is a totality of days
And for each I mouth the words, for Sunday, Monday, and each
Comes and each goes, comes again, from my lips to god's ears,
Tuesday, god's soft ears, the magnificent lobes, the starry canal,
Wednesday. I needn't list them for you. The days within the
Days. In that what is within is at least equal to and perhaps greater
Than what is without. The way between each number is all
The numbers. The interior and exterior, you once called it. It was
Fall. No, early winter, but it might as well have been fall. A Thursday.
Not this early winter, or last, but some early winter. The tender
Leaf cells in danger of rupturing. Unproductive appendages. Each
Posing a threat to the integrity of the tree. The weight of snow. And
So, abscission. The pushing away. "It didn't fall, it was pushed!"
A child laughs. The rake. That final V of geese in the heavens
It would seem, of the dead, so often where they congregate. A
Gathering of angels, of matter. A mattering of angles. The head tilts
Towards the window, more light, and who is this dancing

On the head of my pin? And what of truth, what of consequence,
What of missing the last train to the sea? Of Schuyler quoting
Aeschylus: I forget. Who has the gall to remember? And if remembering
So depends on the rememberer what gaslit stove do I warily
Stoke? Stroke of genius and/ or stroke of a beard and/ or/ or
Not a beard but the way men wore their facial hair back then. Back
When? The street is dry and gray. Fathers sleep in the hills. If
February were May, then what I see now would be leafier. The
Girl says, "After Christmas, should come summer." We should open
Presents then have the ocean. Rifle through stockings then have
Dogdays of reading in hammocks. A palmful of nuts for the
Squirrel. The snowdrops and hailstorms backburnered, and thus
A lid lifted briefly on the spring. Then the moon burns through
And the shadows fall long. The order of things. The long
O of sorrow, sorrowful O of longing. After blood work I took
Sunrise Highway to the ocean, walked out past the dunes, stared
Hard at the eye of the sky, wondered, too, what happens when we
Close our eyes for good. West, you count to sixteen. Lest I've been
Unclear. Lest tested. My winter boots stomped through the snowy
Sand. As though through sandy snow. The wind, a mild hangover. I'll
Tell you everything. The gulls ate the peanut butter sandwich you'd
Packed me. Such beasts, the gulls. Wax paper and all. Foucalt: "The
Great horizontal network forms words from other words and
Propagates them ad infinitum." In such, I drove back to the city in
The slow lane until the slow lane became the only lane. Another
Gull coasts by, unexpected as a kiss on the nape of the neck. These
Birds, these shifts of tense. It flew, and so flies. It is flying and so will
Fly. An ever-presence. The ordinary act made extraordinary by shifting
Lanes. A blinker to signal. The thought of flying, thus flying. I ask

Eva on the way to school if she thinks we carry the memories of
Our ancestors in our cells. She tells me she wants a donut. I ask Ella
On the way home if she knows what an erection is. She says she wants
Mozzarella sticks. So hunger? Distraction? Hamburger thawing in the
Fridge. My flagless, empty mailbox. The morning not even gray yet. Still
Dark ink so that when I look out it's not the trees I see but some version
Of me reflected. Hopper painted *A Woman in the Sun* when his model,
His wife, Josephine was seventy-eight years old. She looks maybe 40.
A very good 40. Was he seeing her, or not seeing her? Having been seen,
Having had been seen. Having had. *Nighthawks. Early Sunday Morning.*
Coasting among the masterpieces, of what use are they? *Angel with a*
Tortoise-shell Comb. Angel in Repose, in Tampa, in Shadow. The blue-gold lilies
To frame. The plush mouth. Triptych of angels. Psyche being woken by
That kiss. To interlock and rotate creating an ascending triangle. The ride
To the bus. Dishes done (they are never done). Time being the canary
In the cul de sac. So many words written and forgotten. The cloud. The
Cold hollow of a spoon. Miles dissolve in a whole valley of green. *Angel*
In a field, a city. Angel with Bowler Hat. I was a child at a strip mall when
I saw her: the trapeze artist with her suntanned-colored tights, her
Wings. If from your garden, you gather firewood, what becomes of the
Apples? *Angel with an Axe. Angel with a Sword.* Angel with the s-word
Hanging slack from his mouth. Silence. The silence after. After what?
After the after. The sizzle and crush of a cigarette under the sky under
An awning under a boot. Incessant daydream. *The First Angel* and *The*
Last. The impermanence of permanence, is that all there is? To look
From one room into the next, the light spilling all over the kitchen
Floor, an open book in a glass case, last year's candles zipped inside
A plastic baggie. What will you wish for? What will you wish you had
Wished for? So hard to find a match these days. Keys, cigarettes, cash.

How you used to stand at the door checking to make sure you had
It all. Now, it's phone, children, dog. Or most days. Most leavings.
A mug filled with pencils. A pair of scissors. I love that they are a
Pair. Like shoes, earrings. A pair of goggles. Of lungs. Eyes. Wings
And chopsticks. Kidneys. Such symmetry between the tape deck
And the moonlight. But then memory and grief. What are the chances
This warm spell will last? It's all a spell, yes? The days sounded
Out. The primary diphthongs, as in, pay, ray, lay. Sky, cry, tie. Come
Lie with me, (that old Ferlinghetti poem). But what I want to say
Is how the light becomes entrapped in a dusty screen, masking out
The view from the porch, from the porch where I snapped beans and
Shucked long ears of tender corn, the silk of which I rubbed on my
Face. The trees. I'd hoped to get to the line of stroking the cat, of
Stroking you as if a cat, but there is a math and an order of things. You
Wake, and it's your birthday again. You read a little while the coffee
Drips from its cone. The long blink, and it's your birthday (again
Again.). Is it luck? Two children come down the stairs. The yellows
And browns of Linder Ave. You slip on a feather, recline on a brown
Leather sofa, your socks still on. I look around my desk for objects I
Might send. "This is something he might like." It was summer. It was
Christmas. It was ice cream dripping from the cone. I was a child. You
Were. Someone had forgotten my birthday, and so from then on, I
Always said, "It's my birthday. This is the day I was born." Mother.
The price of admission to the horrors of civilization. Let's make a list.
A mother forgetting a birthday. A mother not making it to the party. A
Mother not making it to her birthday. The long-stemmed roses. Most
Things are disappearing. That balloon Ella watched float away. That
Any given point in time is not a point. Is that the point? At the
Museum, the guards may only ask you not to touch a painting

again, they cannot ask you not to touch it. The intent itself cannot
Be reprimanded. When I was still in school, Jean would run her hand
Across the page and say, "Here, here is where I feel the heat." One
Big light through the window this morning (I slept in if it can be
Called sleeping in), but such long shadows of my fingers at the
Keyboard. I make a bunny, a horse, maybe more like a dog, though
With intention to make a bird. To fly you the bird. A bit of rage to
Jolt you. The sparrows shake the tree. The third siren of morning
But, too, the silence in which out of the muck arise violet leaves,
And golden, pink tulips, buds tight and how bright they are in this
Light. The nouns. "I'm getting closer to knowing them." This ink
Pen with its little clicker, clickety click, how absently I tell myself
Not to chew it absently, then click click filling the absence in the
Room. "Your absence is a felt presence," I tell my students. Pismo
Beach. Creek and source. The clothespin in your mouth. A line
Stretched from tree to tree. A string with two cans. "Can you
Talk?" And the verbs too. Intransitive. To run to, run from, run
Ragged, runs in the family, a run in my stocking, the train runs from
New York to D.C., the play runs through the weekend, the child
Through the field, fingers through hair, water in the tub. "I always
Knew we'd run out of time:" a woman on the avenue. "I knew
It, knew it, knew it." A brown leaf lets go; a truck beeps in reverse.
To know: what have these years of living and being lived taught us?
A handful of things. How to choose a ripe avocado, how to not
Let bananas go to waste, where to place the star tattoo, and what
Color to make it. "How are you really?" The leaves were falling and
My heart was hurting, or my head, too much gin, but one sleeps
It off, one sleeps and sleeps, if one is lucky, which I rarely am in
That regard. Are you still reading? Have you even begun? My brother

And I were out in the creek. He was getting baptized, or divorced, or
Was drying the dishes with a fresh towel, had thrown the sour one
In the pile to carry to the basement, the fresh towel had lemons, was
Frayed. I want to ask what there is to be scared of, but I know this
Is only one question, and filtered through language, through this
Language, clear as day. It's a little gray. Morning gray. Yellow star
On your forearm. How to sit with uncertainty. Milky sky, a bit of grace
Before waking tremulous hands undo buttons. Another day, the sun
Searching for some bit of equipoise with night; the gardener with his
Shears; those two blades moving on a pin. The purpose of clipping a
Bird's wings is not to render it incapable of flight; flight still comes
To the bird; but lower, in spurts; the clipping ensures it won't fly
Away. Does this difference matter to you? Would it matter if I hadn't
Made it a metaphor? Had I made it a metaphor? That the fire was
First a fire; the blanket a blanket. In the beginning, the pull of the
Tide was only the pull of the tide. A moon's phase. The sky faded
As blue jeans hung on the back of a chair. The air. Hair pinned at
The nape of the neck of a woman you once loved. A mother, a first
Wife, a second. The minutes give way to violins, violets, violence, and
Of harsh reality I would like to interpose: interpose is not the
Word. To place between. To interpose an opaque body between the
Light and the eye. In the midst of conversation, discourse, or the
Like. So, yes, perhaps interpose is the word. And rain. The way it
Collects on the window's screen. The green is coming, at least
Outside. Inside, the plant is nearly dead, and I tell myself to water
It, to water it, then pass it twenty times, thirty. I keep meaning
To ask after the children. To interpose. And of harsh reality (the
Gray) it seems to come anyway. Men came and poured wet
Cement on the block. I thought to write my name, yours, press

My palm, but by the time I got out the door it had hardened, a
Heart, and the clouds came. "Looks like rain:" I've no talent
For tomatoes. Hankerings, yes. A sandwich. I wish I had friends
In California, and they'd box up lemons and send them my way—
Old views and surges of energy or the pure pleasure of
Remembering, the flash across a face, sunlight through the train's
Window and onto the face, then gone again as the tracks bend
Back towards the avenues of Chicago. But before they are gone,
They are there. There. Running one's hands along the fishnet,
Fresh grass. The surface of water. Viscosity. How my brother
Used to slide his socked feet across the carpet then reach his
Fingers to my face to shock me. That jolt. And this winter that
Has been spring all along. February crocuses. I keep thinking it
Will end, and it will end. Change anyway. Those coins on the
Counter. And, too, the honey dripping down the jar. I doubt the
Stars will do much tonight. Sequins in the fog. Is repetition
Boring? Or only those who repeat and repeat themselves? Or not
Boring at all? A comfort. A tisket, a tasket. And how words give
Way to words give way to words give way to other things. It's
The just rightness that counts. And how have you come to know just
What is right? A cool washrag pressed to a warm head. The laundry
Piles up again. Endless. I walk to the river. "How many boys have
Swum in you?!" I who have never put in a toe. Tombstones on the
Shoreline. One, a tome, its very shape. "Book of Life," it
Reads. And what is the book of life? Deadheaded the hydrangeas
Too late maybe to matter, but one tries. Anything for hope. Was
Born, lived, lived well or lived poorly, and likely lived both
Poorly and well, was forgiven, or forgave, went to the source, slipped
Fingers into gloves, filled empty things, emptied full things, slept

In or woke early, rubbed the stain from the shirt until it was
A lighter, larger stain. A basketful of bucket lists. A houseful
Of guests. I had two requests. Do you recall? And then. Then.
Called back. Which is one way of saying it. Shuffled off
The mortal coil. Went home. Went the way of all the earth.
Yet it is not less individual a fate for all that, "When I
Was little," we say, or, "When you were but a glimmer in
Your mother's eye," or, "That was lifetimes ago," when it was
Only a month or so. The ink still wet. A dark beer, and "What
Brings you here?" Here. What does bring me here. A train had
Brought me there, which then brings me here. But a cab to
Catch the train, my willing legs, a heart, a hand to wave down
The cab. Then, too, a little one-lane road surrounded by
Trees. A woman on her knees on a bed. A woman standing
Near the bed. A woman in the sun. A woman in moonlight
Removing her earrings, her watch, hooking her thumb on the
Necklace's latch. All to go in the shallow bedside dish. What phase
Was that night's moon? I'm sure you know. Still, no snow, not
Even much of a chill. Long weekend so no mail. And did I do
The laundry? Must I now again? The tulips drooping prettily,
The rosy violets. Life in action, life in repose, life in
Between the other lifetimes. Calamity and light. Do I think
Each morning when I wake I'll be different? But much the
Same. This robe still. The blow of the steamboat. The sky
Different from yesterday, yes, or I think it will be once the
Sun makes its way around. Different but recognizable, still what
We call sky. They say some are never tested. To which I can
Merely recommend filling all the ovals, a hundred C's filled
With graphite. I think everyone I know must be sleeping in

A bed they'll get up and make or not make. Of things I make,
Weak alfredo and strong coffee included, this is among my
Favorites. This. Also, making do. "You got to dance with
Them what brung you." Sometimes I try to tap into my friends'
Dreams. "Are you sleeping?" I whisper into a sleeping ear.
Ahead, a roadway lined by roses and thunder. "It will be here
Soon, the morning." It will be morning soon, and in your
Father's blue room you will sit drinking what you've poured
From his pot. It will be like a memory. "This is like a memory."
But it will be in accord with time and space. Not a memory
Yet. The pile of bills, his eyeglasses, his handwriting. Had you
Forgotten your father's handwriting? The stars. It was there
All along. The loops of S's and J's, what once was a practiced
Script, now old hat. It was spring when I woke. Magnolias
Melting out front. Thumbnail of a moon. "Where am I?" Not yet
A memory. But the trophies, the large print crossword, three
Cats eating their breakfast from three dishes on the kitchen
Floor. The pattern on china, tiny green leaves. And now your
Father is farther away. Collecting what is his in the back room.
Greenest grass. A funny tree, of many moons, gold in autumn, naked
Come winter. His keys. He puts socks on his wife's feet. It's gotten
Cold again. A rooster. Skylight. It seems I've woken in someone else's
Home. What felt like it would become a memory has become a
Memory. Sharpened colored pencils in a glass coffee mug. A cat on my
Chest at dawn. "Guten morgen, Katze." All the things to know and
Not know, to say and not say. I write a note to myself on a bright
Yellow square. "Remember this." Tiny glass rabbits and loose
Tea leaves. Someone else's thirst, their delight, the sound of rain on
Their windowpane. So much to follow, and so little. What will happen

Next. The order. The ordering. Someone else's book. Their dog
Eared chapter. As if one could actually choose one's adventure. Bubble
Gum in the hair, Jesus Saves in the parking lot. And then, we do it
All again. Light the candle. Blow it out. Light the candle. And middle
Age like a borrowed shirt with a missing button. Or a half dozen
Buttons in a blue bowl, origin unknown. The rooster again, after a
Dreamless sleep, to be mindless and at one with all that grows,
Mindless, the knowing without knowing, what the bones feel when
Wind comes through the valley. What did you wish for? For what
Did you wish? What did you wish? Did you? What do I and did
I and what is it to wish? The tulips open. For now, the music of
The ceiling fan. On the mountain, we ran out of beer so wake with
No hangover, no regret, no particular place to point, to say, "This
Is what I did wrong. This is where I went wrong." Take a right
At the three dilapidated crosses, the directions read, and they
Stood gasping at the edge of the ditch. Silver-white, more stone than
Wood, but wood. Cold water in a Ball jar. I'll leave this place soon
Enough, take the left, get elsewhere, leave there. The permanence
Of impermanence. A thumbtack on a map. How are your thumbs,
Throat, the insides of your wrists. Are you still in winter. Are you
Down. Unhibernate. Let the rain soak your hair, run down your
Face, swim in your jugular notch, drip down your sternum, flatten
The pelt of your belly. This morning, windchimes and thrushes,
The happy trail down to the river where my grandmother caught
Crawdads, was baptized, cleaned her dishes and herself, necked
With a boy she loved. The stitching on blue jeans and the dog
Mouth pink of the cherry trees. All things being equal, though
None of them are. A bucket banging on the side of a shin, the
Sunburned shoulders, a textbook example. The cirrus composed

Entirely of ice crystals. Feather and wisp. The first sign of a
Warm front. Also, what I see from the porch this morning, or
Some morning, as this morning will soon be. I send ardor and
Sympathy. Thank you, May, for these warm stirrings. Life
With its uncountable nouns, its patterns and pattering, March
Coming as March comes. How many Marches? And the Marches
Within each March. Februaries within Februaries. If we are
Quiet. If we find quietness. Another mountain. "The highway
Runs both ways." Soon enough, August in the East. But May, M,
May I call you, M, May, may I call you, M? "Behave yourself." The
Children on the pallet lined up like fish sticks. Being eleven and
Far from museums. Far from that light, but in this light. How the
Light travels. "You brought the spring." Now, shake the petals
From your hair, and get on with it. It was the day after I turned
Ten, and the boy said, "Your birthday is the farthest away," and I
Said, "No, it was yesterday," and he said, "But yesterday is
Gone." How we wait and wait, until we are no longer waiting. In
A dishpan the soap powder dissolves under a turned-on faucet and
Another wedding is emptied of its California light. The buzz of
Champagne, flies. The bowl left sticky with melon. Hopper's
Wife, her nipples and her fortitude. Best to throw out the old
Blue sponge. Start again. Hot water from the spigot. To transpose
Is its own sort of imposition. But the tulips, the plant I finally
Remember, carry water from last night's pot, deliver from the
Brink, turn a quarter to catch sun. Life, I do not understand. The
Days tick by, each so unique, each so alike: what is that chatter
Beneath the window? The scrape of shovels. A neighbor with a
Box of pears. And the panes of glass. Blue beside blue, what I
Might send you, what you might receive. A piece of mail arrives

On a Sunday before sunrise. It is the unexpected, the tangle, and
Tuesday again. Blow by blow, until we are so solidly in the middle
Of our lives we may as well be near the end. O improbable
Yellow, speck of lint on a sweater in a photograph. The particulars
Of this living in this body. What I haven't said I haven't said. What
I'll say I'll say. The nouns and verbs disappear, water under the
Bridge. Under the breath. Thick as stone this panic and enchantment,
This blood. The order of things shaking, shook. What I mistook,
And all which was not mistaken. "Forsake me not." O Air. "Why
Ask questions?" and, "What are the questions you wish to ask?"

The Examination

How Does Your Body Feel Right Now?

Like I've waded into an aboveground pool in a Target bathing suit.
Like I'm a European man with dry mouth.
Like I want to put my fingers somewhere.
Like I wonder if that thigh-chaffing butter-stick works.
Like I've got to pee out these two glasses of Kombucha.
Come closer.
Like I reek of Tampa.
Like a swallow of wine.
Come even closer.
Like I am standing in an elementary school talking to other mothers about snacks.
Like I need mouthwash.
Like I need someone to slap me.
Closer still.
Like a radiant pig.
Now, stay.

How Does Your Central Nervous System Feel Right Now?

I was just thinking, what if I do have satin walls?
What if I do love cranes?
I think probably I am THE ENEMY.
But I like you.
Usually, the chain around my ankle embarrasses me.
A ring of eczema where my ring should be.

Also, under the bridge, the snake eating the bluegill.
I was hungry, too.
Am, I should say, am. Will be.
But a not-wife, I am not.
Throat knot. Heart knot. What-not.
I've draped my wet pants over the radiator.
And I swear I will not cry publically.
Not here. Not today.

And Your Brain, How Does it Feel?

Funny that you ask.
It feels like billions of nerve cells arranged in patterns to coordinate
thought, emotion, behavior, movement, and sensation.
An egg frying on a pan.
Sheet music.
An egg in a nest.
An egg being pushed out of a bird.
Getting laid by?
A bird.
My mother (still radiant) when they took her.
A slapped face slapped again.
That painting with its sky.
The broken shell of a robin's blue egg clinging to my thumbnail.

True Story w/ Goat

My husband says, you can drop a goat on the moon, go back five years later, and it'll still be kicking around. Tough fuckers, he says. I gnaw on a sheet of cardboard while he talks. The nickel moon shines on the little bed of newspaper and dandelions that I've made in the corner. What you likely don't know about me is that my intestines are made of catgut and used to make internal human stitches and the strings of musical instruments. Meaning: I will play you a song while I heal your secret wound. When we married, I said *I do* with my slit-shaped pupils, and he promised to never remove my horns to make spoons. But you know how time is: it's got a four-chambered stomach. The point, he says, is that goats don't need shit to live. He clangs what was once mine into his cereal bowl, and I bury my head into his thigh, bleating, which sounds like a screaming human, but is really just the only way I know how to make sound.

all the good poems these days

seem to be about caves   and ladies hunkering down in them
or groping around the wet dark opening   I tell my students
if you run your hand along the wall for long enough
you'll probably find a light switch   but I tell them all sorts of things
tonight Eva is riding on a Zamboni   I like how Zamboni
rhymes with pony and I like the dusk and the way
it gets dark so early   that's a lie   now I will tell you lies
all the good poems these days tell lies   not really   that's a lie
is it   it is   is it   I haven't been in a cave in years   actually
I'm not sure I've ever been in a cave or if I'm remembering
watching *Goonies* in the half-light   I have a memory of riding
horses in the snow in South Dakota   the pines buckled
my crotch ached   my mother says it never happened
and by it I mean everything   everything never happened
nothing ever happened   these days poets say they want to curse
in all their poems and talk about politics and some other poets say
they have no desire for syntax or sex because the world is so
and then they curse and point towards the sky   in high school
this girl abby said she was trying to get her bf to do her
but he kept pointing to the ceiling   god she asked is it god
but he was talking about her parents upstairs sleeping
or maybe not sleeping maybe just listening for the sound
of their daughter not being done   being undone   today for lunch
I packed Ella shrimp cocktail and three tiny apples   all the good
poems these days have shrimps   I tell Zoë I wish I could write
poems for my daughters   also I'm going to tell you now
because I keep forgetting to tell anyone in real life

so all I have is this life but what I'm going to tell you is that
I've seen three shooting stars in the past month   this makes me
think that either something really good is about to happen
or the sky is bottoming out   in china fireflies are harvested
and you can buy tickets to go to the park and watch their lights
what I'm asking is would you like to buy a ticket   all the good poems
these days sell tickets   if you buy this one I'll rub your temples
and sing you a song and nobody will never have to know

August, still

Born, I cried,
and growing, I cried.
Gathering the broken egg, I cried.
Making the pancakes, eating the pancakes,
cleaning up after the pancakes, I cried.
Watching you swim to the deep area, I cried.
Watching you return to the shallows, I cried.
When my husband could not love me
like I wanted, I cried.
When I could not love my husband
as he needed, I cried.
When we loved each other anyway, I cried.

And then, there was the pulling of the weeds,
which I did all morning, crying,
and the watching them return,
which I did all afternoon, crying.
Now, evening, and what am I to do
but pull the weeds again,
and let the mosquitos suck on me,
and watch the stars come out, one by one?

dwelling

that winter it was so cold
I had nowhere to go but inside

my heart was a clock on the kitchen wall
and I tacked up curtains to keep

anyone from looking in on my liver
up river snow kept coming

and the aching thing ached still
husband it was yours for the taking

I clanged pots against my radiator thighs
duct-taped my mouth all the doors

if only we could lose the hour
if only we could witness a single bloom

listen if spring ever comes
I will open these windows to you

and beat this old rug of a soul clean
the house will be pristine

and I will be your wife again

Marriage

& of the lattermath I can only say
that with the rain the cattails grew so high
that the longing nearly subsided
this morning I am all moonshine on the snowbank
clockwise back to a better self I am
tenderfoot daisywheel though yesterday I was
warpath and daydreams of underfoot animals
o my fishhook in sheepskin I want
to spacewalk in time with you to teaspoon
sugar into your mouth to clean horsehairs
from under your fingernails honeymoon
of the longhouse I'll meet you on the shadyside
of the limestone for years I grew lukewarm
with a backache but now I am whitefish
and blackberries I am forbearer and undercurrent
buttermilk and motherhood watertight thunderbird
forgive me my wipeout my deadend and foremost
forgive me my butterball my washrag wrung out
the grasslands of the graveyard I nearly misrecognized
what I almost became eggshell watercolor
drained pipe goodbye o my forever bedclothes
yours is the body warmblooded washbowl
that I seahorse into night after night and the dogwood
timepiece ticks the gumball fruitcup earache of our girls
you my wavelength my tailbone lemon jellybean
crewcut backstroke beachcomber I do I do

Jan. 10

Please receive this that I send you. Please accept my apologies for the
insufficiency of language: metaphor wilts. Understand that I mostly see
the body as body but for our purposes it will be both sentence and flower.
Please note that the body as sentence is a fragment and that I have circled
with my red pen all the spaces that lack completeness. Please also accept
these irises that I tore them from the earth; place them in hot water. Please
note first the red circle around the thighs. I have been having heaviness in
my chest; it will be embarrassing to die. Please dismiss the image of my
daughters sleeping like commas, the coma of my husband in the far room
among the flowers. Red halo of the brain is most obvious. Haloed heart
promotes cliché. Please clean your fingernails of dirt. Clip the stem of me.
And when my syntax fails, please press me into an unwanted book so that,
in one hundred years, I may fall on a stranger's feet.

The Cat is Black

or what someone said Vievee Francis says to write when you reach a wall

Reader, having reached the wall,
and finding the cat, black,
and the frigate stalled in the harbor,
and my mother, whom I've worshiped,
though with complications, sneezing
in Oklahoma, or only in the poem,
sneezing, the spray spreading blue
ink, the sallow font, reader, without
pretense, I say, I have loved, and been
loved, reader, but what to do after
the acknowledgement? The cat is black,
and I've yet to eat. The cat is black,
and the tiny violin plays its sad song.
The cat is black, and the cashmere bleating,
which is to say, I've made this thing
from the living thing. I've lived
and made the thing, reader, and what more
might I mention? There is nothing new,
Nothing is new, and it's nearly a new year.
Only the year is new, and New York City.
I am reckless with the arcane. I am not
the first hungry woman, not even
in this poem am I the first hungry woman,
but god, the hunger, reader, and the cat
with the broken spine dragging itself
to the back room to die alone. My brother,
afternoons, boiled the skin off raccoons,
and I steal this too. It was not my water

that boiled. These are not my walls,
reader, nor does the cat belong to anyone,
not even itself, or does it? Z says she stood
in the shower and patted down her body.
This is the space that I inhabit, she said.
Meanwhile, I smell the stench in my robe.
Meanwhile, the cancer drugs, the paper cuts.
The little bowl of milk I leave out
for the cat, should he choose to return.

The End of the Pier

I walked to the end of the pier
and threw your name into the sea,
and when you flew back to me—
a silver fish—I devoured you,
cleaned you to the bone. I was through.
But then you came back again:
as sun on water. I reached for you,
skimmed my hands over the light of you.
And when the sky darkened,
again, I thought it was over, but then,
you became water. I closed my eyes
and lay on top of you, swallowed you,
let you swallow me too. And when
you carried my body back to shore—
as I trusted that you would do—
well, then, you became shore too,
and I knew, finally, I would never be through.

Having Purged

Or maybe purged is the wrong word.
Having taken spaghetti into my throat.
Having been wife. Been made wife.
Been hunter, but also hunted. Having
chilled so many bottles of the white stuff.
Having pulled the shades, the wild card,
the wool, the pretty shirt with the tiny roses
over my head. Having a ball. The gall.
Having been so casual. Having trace
amounts of blood, of protein, of gold,
leukocytes, ketones. Having wished
for something I already have. Having
told X why, and ridden to the hospital
in the cold. Having a body. A vagina.
Language. Having utter discombobulation.
A skeleton carrying a birthday cake.
Having been to the lake. What's missing?
What is the mourned thing? The glass
on the bedside table, the bruise on the knee
that was unknowingly knocked. I tell
you there was something upside down.
A gutted fish on a paper dish. To vocalize
would be to say this thing or that. To tell
one woman's truth, to stand at an outpost,
on a threshold, on a cafeteria table,
to be able to say. And having said
to not be made alone. Having longing.
Having been given the switch. Having

ancestors and wreckage. It feels so silly
to come to the page. A modern calamity.
Stolen offering. Something about karma,
about being sorry. The curry fries.
About heaving, cleaving. The heave
and ho, the cleaving to. A drink at the mall.
And man the binge which preceded it all.

Birthday

In the middle of my fifth decade, there were so many rooms.

Catfish room of my girlhood where I'd throw nets.

Fishnet room of my twenties where I'd run my hands.

There was a room filled with hearts, both human and animal.

Your heart was there, of course, throbbing, warm.

Mostly, old friends walked through my dreams.

Hillery with her dog, Jane along the beach.

Zoë and I wrote of how there were more days gone than coming.

We thought we were okay with this, but maybe we weren't.

The whistle of the steam train blew.

There were choices I had made which were poor.

But then, there were plenty which seemed to indicate wisdom.

I knew I wanted cake, so was happy to have a cake room.

Also, most of the rooms had windows, and I like light.

I had gained a little weight, but, still, was sleeping.

I wondered if I would soon descend into melancholia.

In the candle room, I counted forty-five candles.

And when I wanted something to grow on, I counted another.

I needed to call my mother back.

I didn't want my mother ever to die.

She had given birth to me forty-five years before.

Giving birth is excruciatingly painful.

For a long while, it seemed better not to name things.

But then, I wanted to give everything a name.

The desire room, the comfort room, the husband room.

There are poems I want to be read at my funeral.

In the heart room are the hearts of two cats I left for dead.

I still feel bad about that, and other things.

I hope that I have not been too unkind.

Kristin boils eggs that we will later eat.

I tend to start in the past and move to the present.

I tell my students I need space.

Press the Enter key, I say.

I press the Enter key.

I will go for a swim, even though I do not swim.

I will sing a song, even though I do not sing.

There is a fucking room and a weeping room.

There is a room where I do nothing but fold laundry.

I will write you a letter today and press flowers into it.

It will be so sad, for a little while, when one of us dies.

We will be like, wait, it is Sunday, where are you?

But then another will die, and another.

After a while, it won't be sad anymore.

It will just be the way that things are.

There is a room where things are just as they are.

I am there now. I write myself a birthday poem,

and then, I open the windows to let in more air.

Acknowledgements

Academy of American Poets poets.org: "The End of the Pier" and "Marriage"

American Poetry Review: "dwelling"

The Arts Fuse: "Time"

Copper Nickel: "Jan. 10"

Dialogist: selections from "some psalms"

DIODE: "Hymn to Life"

Elsewhere: "True Story w/ Giraffe"

The Equalizer: "Summertime Sundries"

Foundry: "Girlhood"

GRIST: "How We Flounder Here on Earth"

Lunch Ticket: "The Examination"

Mississippi Review: "True Story w/ Goat"

Missouri Review: "Having Purged"

Muzzle: "all the good poems these days"

Parenthesis: "Morning"

PEN America: "The Stick"

Plume: "Snow: An Essay"

Poetry Northwest, "twenty"

Rise-Up Review: "The Origin of Birds"

Sixth Finch: excerpts from "Aging, "The Cat is Black," and "On the Second Day of the Third Decade in the 21st Century"

SF&D: "Diction"

Southern Indiana Review: "The Ratchet"

The Shallow Ends: "True Story w/ Horse"

SWWIM: "August, still"

The Tiny: "Beachcombing at 44"
Tin House: "Burrow"
Typo: "Birthday"
West Trestle: "Twenty-two"
Yes, Poetry: "Aging" (chapbook)

For their generosity, inspiration, and decades of writerly friendship, deep thanks to Russell Carmony, Kristin Dombek, Lorraine Doran, Iris Jamahl Dunkle, Stephanie Hopkins, Ada Limón, Dawn Lundy Martin, Caitlin McDonell, Matthew Nicholas, Sanjana Nair, and Zoë Ryder White. For early editorial insight, Sean Singer and Sherine Gilmour. For their mind-blowing word games and loud ass laughter, the Women of the Matrix. For the day in and day out of nearly every day, my Poetry Club & my Google Doc companions. I love you all!

For her acumen and care, I'm grateful to my editor, Sarah Wetzel.

To my family: inexpressible thanks to my mother, father, stepmother, and stepfather. To my daughters, Eva and Ella, who bring me the deepest joy I know. And finally, to my husband, Cody, whose unwavering love continually grants me the space to live and write and be.

Notes

"some psalms" uses Robert Alter's translation of *The Book of Psalms* as a starting point.

"Summertime Sundries" was copied from my journal one summer and may contain unattributed lines to writers I admire.

"Hymn to Life" was written in a February 2023 postcard exchange with Michael Robins. Approximately every fourteenth line is taken from James Schuyler's poem of the same title.

About the Author

Nicole Callihan is the author of *chigger ridge,* winner of the Tenth Gate Prize, *This Strange Garment*, *SuperLoop*, the 2019 novella, *The Couples*, as well as several chapbooks. A frequent collaborator with artists around the world, she has received support from the Rockefeller Foundation, Bethany Arts, Ludwig Vogelstein, and the Sustainable Arts Foundation. Originally from Hickory, North Carolina, she now lives in Miami.

Also by Nicole Callihan

chigger ridge

This Strange Garment

SuperLoop

The Couples

Slip was printed in Adobe Caslon Pro
www.saturnaliabooks.org